The Beauty of Vultures

POEMS BY WENDY McGRATH

The Beauty of Vultures

PHOTOS BY DANNY MILES

NeWest Press

Library and Archives Canada Cataloguing in Publication
Title: The beauty of vultures / poems by Wendy McGrath ; photographs by Danny Miles.
Names: McGrath, Wendy, author | Miles, Danny, photographer.
Series: Crow said poetry.
Description: Series statement: Crow said poetry
Identifiers: Canadiana (print) 20240463382 | Canadiana (ebook) 20240464567 | ISBN 9781774391129 (softcover) | ISBN 9781774391136 (EPUB)
Subjects: LCGFT: Poetry. | LCGFT: Illustrated works.
Classification: LCC PS8575.G74 B43 2025 | DDC C811/.6 — dc23

NeWest Press wishes to acknowledge that the land on which we operate is Treaty 6 territory and Métis Nation of Alberta Region 4, a traditional meeting ground and home for many Indigenous Peoples, including Cree, Saulteaux, Niitsitapi (Blackfoot), Métis, Dene, and Nakota Sioux, since time immemorial.

Editors for the Press: Thea Bowering and Jumoke Verissimo
Cover and interior design: Natalie Olsen, Kisscut Design
Cover photography: (front) © Kim Swain/Stocksy.com, (back) © Danny Miles

Canada Council for the Arts | Conseil des Arts du Canada | Funded by the Government of Canada | Financé par le gouvernement du Canada | Canada

NeWest Press acknowledges the support of the Canada Council for the Arts, the Government of Alberta through the Ministry of Arts, Culture and Status of Women and the Edmonton Arts Council for support of our publishing program. We acknowledge the financial support of the Government of Canada through the Canada Book Fund for our publishing activities.

NEWEST PRESS

NeWest Press
#201, 8540-109 Street
Edmonton, Alberta T6G 1E6
www.newestpress.com

No bison were harmed in the making of this book.
Printed and bound in Canada
1 2 3 4 25 26 27 28

FOR JOHN —WENDY

FOR CELINE CLERMONT —DANNY

contents

intro

WENDY McGRATH:

Danny Miles and I were well into the collaborative project that would become *The Beauty of Vultures* when he asked me, "Can you write a poem about an owl?"

It was November 18, 2018, and Danny was recording with July Talk at The Bathouse — The Tragically Hip's recording studio on the shore of Lake Ontario. Gord Downie had passed a little over a year before this session and Danny told me how emotional it was for him to be there. On a break that day, he ventured out into the snow with his camera thinking he might take some photographs and clear his head. He described an unexpected encounter with an owl resting on a fence post near the highway — and Danny took it as a sign. It wasn't difficult for me to imagine this chance meeting for the drummer who loves birds. The photograph Danny shared with me inspired the poem "At the Bathouse: November 18, 2018" which was displayed beside his photograph in an exhibition at the 2019 Junos in London, Ontario — Danny's hometown. It was a moment when birds, photography, music, and poetry converged and there have been many such moments for me as Danny and I worked on this project.

The idea for *The Beauty of Vultures* began in 2017. My eldest son, musician and writer Eamon McGrath, a good friend of Danny's, told me about the drummer's, then, new-found passion for birding and bird photography. I began following Danny's work on social media — #drummerswholovebirds — and was captivated and inspired by his images. Here were photographs that reached me on multiple levels, and the more I looked at Danny's photographs, the more apparent it seemed to me that we should work together on a project of some kind. I reached out to Danny, inviting him to collaborate and, initially, he sent me several of his then-favourite photographs — a molting male peacock, a juvenile great blue heron, a pair of egrets, a cardinal resting on a branch, a northern harrier. I'm not sure what he expected would result from this back-and-forth, but I spent time with these images and wrote some of the first pieces for what would become *The Beauty of Vultures*. Danny liked those early pieces and sent me more photographs. Rather than simply writing call-and-response ekphrastic poems, I let the photographs guide me to places beyond mere description. They became portals. I saw multiple connections — to other genres, artists; such as Rothko and Egon Schiele, poets; such as Gwendolyn MacEwen and W.H. Auden, folklore, mythology, superstitions, dance, tarot, and nursery rhymes. I pushed beyond a simple call-and-response, experimenting with form I felt was often suggested by a photograph — the sonnet, pantoum, acrostic, ghazal, concrete poem, incantation, and even a mini-play. I discovered how birds are seen as possible links between the real and supernatural — messengers and harbingers. Danny's photographs also evoked strong memories for me. My name could indeed have been Robin, I remembered the air-raid drills we still had when I first started school, I see the dangers and threats in the world we're living in and the Pandemic we endured. All this came about by Danny introducing me to his love of birds. Now I am one of those #writerswholovebirds and look toward the sky. (I am currently trying to befriend some crows who visit our backyard, leaving them bits of cheese, making sure they know I'm friend not foe...)

What began as a suite of ekphrastic poems and photographs evolved into a collection of poetic experiments in form and approach and photographs that demonstrate Danny's talent in an artform outside his music. He joins the ranks of other artists who excel at more than one discipline – poet/musician/artist Joni Mitchell, musician and renowned mycologist John Cage, poet/photographer Philip Larkin, and jazz pianist Bill Evans – who had quite the talent for betting on horses.

Writing is such a solitary activity and my collaborations with other artists and musicians confirms my belief that we need more cross-pollination between genres; it enriches our artistic and literary landscape and broadens our experiences – of art, music, and of being part of a supportive community. It has been a pleasure and privilege to work with Danny Miles on *The Beauty of Vultures*. We see this project evolving beyond the page, with Danny recording some of the pieces in this collection, setting them to music as part of his solo work. Immerse yourself in this book – birds, poetry, photography, and music have so much to give us.

DANNY MILES:

Many people find it strange and fascinating that I got into bird photography. For me, it was something that happened naturally; it almost found me — as clichèd as that sounds. I have always had an interest in birds, especially birds of prey. It was never something people would have noticed, though, because music was my true passion, even as a child. I was always playing air guitar, using a tennis racquet as guitar, or being the centre of attention at a wedding by dancing to Michael Jackson. Music has always been a huge part of my life and still is: it's what I do for a living. I always think about how lucky I am that my passion, my music, has become my full-time job. Now bird photography, my new passion, is starting to shape my life in a different way.

Birding is very different than playing music. But, for me, they each influence the other. The chaos of the music industry — touring, playing, rehearsing — generates my need to take a breath, to go out and take photos of birds, in part for the good of my mental health. The relaxation of bird photography inspires me to be creative in music because it allows me to think clearly and focus on what art I want to make without feeling stressed or worried. The process helps get my mind off a ridiculous grudge, or some other thing that doesn't really matter. In music, ego can get in the way, and ego isn't a factor when I'm birding and taking photographs.

I really enjoy my time alone, going hiking or running; just being on my own is something I have always enjoyed. There is also a side of me that loves people and being around them. This contradiction is where my passion for performing music and taking pictures of birds makes sense. I think it was while I was touring in Florida with July Talk, just walking around, that I really realized birds and nature were inspiring me. I was walking through a neighbourhood and two sandhill cranes were on a front lawn; they were large and so fascinating to me. Something happened to me at that moment and the idea of birding was something I couldn't get out of my head. I still can't explain it. I sometimes now find myself standing in a line for coffee at an airport on my way home from a tour, probably tired, and wondering why birds are so important to me and thinking it might seem a bit weird that I do bird photography; but, I legitimately get excited when I leave my house to head to take bird photos. It's exciting because I have no idea what I will see.

I have had so many special moments with nature when I have been out birding and it's not always simply about the birds. I've had a deer spy on me through the bush just a couple feet away while I was looking for a bird I was trying to take a photo of. The deer and I made eye contact and we both were fascinated with each other, not scared but curious. These are the amazing moments I look forward to out in nature. I admit I've been a little careless: like the time a rattlesnake crossed my path in California while I was out taking photos. I literally crouched down to its level to take the picture while it was moving towards me — not caring that this thing could kill me, or at least put me in a hospital. (Pretty stupid, I know!)

I mentioned before that my bird photography seemed to develop organically, and this book came together in the same way. As well as playing in July Talk and producing my solo music, I also play drums sometimes with a guy named Eamon McGrath. He is an incredible talent, maybe the most underrated song writer in Canada and beyond. Through Eamon, Wendy McGrath was introduced to my photography.

Wendy and I had heard of each other, but we had never met. She started commenting on bird photos I was posting on social media; she seemed to really like them. Her perspective was unique and it fascinated me. The comments she wrote about my photos were always so well-written and creative, and they made me smile. She told me they inspired her. Wendy approached me about a book-length collaborative project in which she would write poetry inspired my bird photography. At first, I was skeptical; but quickly, once I saw an example of her vision, I was all for this project and making it happen. Out of this, a book was born. But more importantly, a friendship was born — as odd as our friendship may seem, maybe as odd as a wild musician doing bird photography, I suppose. We hope you enjoy this book and hope it inspires you to be weird and creative. The world needs more of that.

PASO DOBLE

A MESSAGE FROM THE PEAHEN TO THE PEACOCK

You trained your blue and green hundred-eyed tail
on me because you wanted me to choose.
I've seen that gaudy display too often.
Hardly registers: stirs nothing in me.

Your tail's molted, turned to bolted-shut eye. That makes me care.
It's your song that interests me now. C'mon.
Sing me a song before or after. It's
a peahen's pick. Peahen to my peacock.

You pulled Hera's chariot
and I fancy that's no feather weight tale.
Your crest is more like flowers than feathers.
Take off your hat and I'll catch the bouquet.

> Your tail opened with too many cock eyes.
> I said close your eyes. Close your fucking eyes.

A BARN SWALLOW RELATIVE TO OBJECTS AND PLACES

you are the weight of
one house key
two pencils
20 paper clips

you build your nest in
barn
bridge
culvert

because you want humans
to hear you above their pointless noise
an open mouth is your default position
to sing to eat or yawn.

I turn my house key in the lock, open my mouth to shout to an empty house
where I keep two pencils in a hand-blown glass cup made by my son
with 20 paper clips that have magnetized all on their own.
I swallow this emptiness and simply shape my hands into a nest.

PASO DOBLE

water ringing in double time
a mirror image now in perfect step
its own mirage startled
this flustered great egret, stopped
light-snapped a blue sweeping cape
this fisher, sword-beaked bully
glass to water turning heron blue
light in their dance, twinning, bending neon

a neon-bender's twinning, this dance in light
that blue heron turning water to glass
a bully of a sword fisher
its sweeping cape snapped light
that stopped a great egret
flustered by its own mirage
a misstep, a mirror image
double time in rings of water

THE HARRIER'S EYE

that reflection, a past life
born and reborn many times
my flight marks a circle, my body a V
feather to bone and bone to beak

born and reborn many times
hawk hieroglyph and king
feather turns to bone and curved beak
believe what the photograph tells you

hawk hieroglyph and king
calls past and the future
believe what the photograph tells you
but you will never capture me

calls past and the future
I am the bird you covet
but you will never catch me
between sky and earth

I am the bird you covet
the music you hear before you wake
between sky and earth
the music you hear before you die

the music you hear before you wake
is that reflection in my eye
the music you hear before you die
a drumbeat you somehow already know

my flight marks a circle, my body a V
a past life, that reflection

THE CROOKED BUSH

This grove of aspen trees is a
botanical mystery.
It is a natural treasure, therefore,
we ask that you treat it with
respect.

FRIENDS OF THE CROOKED BUSH

Under cloud cover we finally find the crooked bush in a farmer's field
and I'm not sure if it's the beginning, end, or middle of nowhere.

The trees read like undesirable Scrabble letters K F Y W and cleft and dive
toward Hafford, Saskatchewan twisting to ground going nowhere.

Not buried treasure or family treasure not even the kind of trees you might sing songs about
this grave natural treasure of aspens snakes in the tall grass on its way to nowhere.

A tree bends over backward on the boardwalk we tread with my dog on a leash
so I take a picture and a wasp nest's angry murmurations attack from nowhere.

A nest of baby birds, open-mouthed little gargoyles, guards the door of a bleached-wood outhouse.
Wendy, it's a mystery how you manage to find a bathroom, even in the middle of nowhere.

THE GOLDFINCH CHARM

is more than
a song, passion that transforms purple thistledown
into spun threads of dragon's beard candy

is more than
a song, passion that turns with the leaves
falling like your feathers to an undercoat of yellow

is more than
a song, passion that sounds with sweet orange
whistling down our birth, our life, our death

SPARROW

Sparrow on a fence
prow on a fence
sparrow on a fence
spare row on a fence
sparrow on a fence
spare **O** on a fence
sparrow on a fence
bare row faded fence
sparrow on a fence
barrow sentry on a fence
sparrow on a fence
souls on defense

FALLING ASLEEP READING STEPHEN KING

In the murky second before I woke
to Kiri te Kanawa singing
Doretta's Dream, I reached toward
the blue shadow on the back of a white swan.

It swam away from me transformed.
A female swan is a pen and eyes open
I try to write this dream:
a moment stolen or given.

I couldn't tell if it was
winter or summer
day or night.
I had seen my half-life.

A young brown swan
had passed in silence.

HOLLY IN THE VIOLET BED

I like children who believe in fairy tales,
I met my first elf under a rosebush.
Quaker ladies frost the meadow with stars,
watch for my sweet unicorn to come cropping violets.

One Tuesday not long ago,
music played on some ancient stringed instrument.
The house breathes lilac,
winter off somewhere leaving milk untouched.

Teddy found
Santa Claus on the roof.
Holly in the violet bed by the well,
sorry for folk who never meet a unicorn.

Turn a switch,
the country is heading for disaster.

Found/redacted/manipulated poem from "Butternut Wisdom," Gladys Taber, *Family Circle Magazine*, May 1966.

AUTUMN

children gone grieving
scrub grass green patched with brown
the hare quickly turns

turns quickly and the hare
brown patches in green scrub grass
grieving gone children

STILLS

1. Hülda
You can't fly home on one wing.
There's no such thing as one last drink.
Well water clear and clean and hooch
drunk from mason jars. 80 proof. A secret still
hidden in the bush where Mounties wouldn't see
when they came searching for proof.

2. Friederich
Outside the family his story was told:
You know how cold it gets 'round Christmastime.
So he stacked bales around the exhaust pipe of his truck.
A nest of straw. Neat. Tidy. Snug. Warm.
He just wanted to keep himself warm, eh? Still kept the truck running.
Wife and eleven kids. It was an accident.
He must've been cold.

3. Hülda
The sleeves of the white shirt draped the board
wings bluing as night came to her kitchen
lifting quietly as she pushed the heavy iron
back and forth.

She was still. Waiting
to lift the second iron heating
on the stove she touched
the shirt sleeves and they lifted
like wings.

Hülda dreamed she was a white bird
with strength to fly home.

4. Hülda
She had carried tiny black poppy seeds in a muslin pouch
tucked in her case with no idea where she would plant
these beautiful and useful red flowers soft, sweet opening
to summer in a strange place.

In winter's wings she put the baby to sleep trickling tea
steeped from those seeds into his open little mouth
to keep him still.

THE HANGED MAN

GULLED

> *Unendowed with wealth or pity,*
> *Little birds with scarlet legs,*
> *Sitting on their speckled eggs,*
> *Eye each flu-infected city.*
>
> "THE FALL OF ROME," W.H. AUDEN

one man shoots a gun and executes a faraway atrocity
here, smart bombs and bullets
while inhuman hurricanes with human names
start the race toward superlatives
used by a president in a hierarchy of disasters
along crowded sidewalks and streets
over and over all caps contain the crowd
DO NOT CROSS DO NOT CROSS DO NOT CROSS
waiting to activate article 50
Unendowed with wealth or pity.

now every news item seems a set warning:
contains violence and upsetting scenes
a gull perched on the head of a parched wooden eagle
meditates on macabre taxidermy
steampunk gerbils or an animal-head balloon
a red-footed tortoise with the head of a kitten
and how not so long ago live freak shows were *de rigueur*
when dead wax figures travelled with the carnival
dreaming of becoming an allegory in a painting of
Little birds with scarlet legs.

ANTHROPOCENE! Did you begin
with the steam engine's revolution of soot
the testing 1-2-3 of radioactive symmetry
the chicken or its egg the tip of a melting iceberg?
dozing toward the next extinction
fed with sugar and salt
birds die on the beach gutted by plastic
and well-heeled holiday-makers stretch out and tan their legs
Sitting on their speckled eggs.

our souls become birds when we die
so the gull with its red beak and red legs
now dreams of killing antibiotic-resistant pathogens
staphylococcus streptococcus enterobacteria
but the bird's imagined ambitions
become suspicions
of dropping feathers and
remembrance of avian epidemics
with webbed feet splayed on a weathered pier the gull will
Eye each flu-infected city.

REDBIRD

30 strike anywhere pocket wood matches matches wood pocket anywhere strike 30

30 strike anywhere pocket wood wood pocket anywhere strike 30

30 strike anywhere pocket pocket anywhere strike 30

30 strike anywhere anywhere strike 30

30 strike strike 30

30 30

0 Keep away from children 0

30 30

30 strike strike 30

30 strike anywhere anywhere strike 30

30 strike anywhere pocket pocket anywhere strike 30

30 strike anywhere pocket wood wood pocket anywhere strike 30

30 strike anywhere pocket wood matches matches wood pocket anywhere strike 30

AIR RAID SIREN

in the elementary school yard
the air raid siren was a giant bird
with its metal bones its long steel legs
its territory bordered by a chain-link fence

the siren was a reminder:
we were nesting in the winged shadow of WWII
and practiced evacuation drills imagining birds falling from the sky,
too many to ever count

I counted on our robins to return every spring
pulling worms, then to a nest decorated with red string
I waited for their blue eggs to break open
climbed the tree to see the still-blind babies

but the nest held
only empty shells

DUCKS IN A ROW

That yellow rubber duck is my surreal mythology.
Head above water. Stay calm. Paddle like crazy. Make like a duck.

My grandfather in a photo squeezing the neck of that dead bird.
I watched as my grandmother gutted and plucked the duck.

An enigmatic decoy sleeps while accordion polka music plays.
Can't these birds tell decoys are fake? Poor sitting duck.

Wooden duck calls wait by the phone like renaissance instruments.
I don't believe what looks like a duck and quacks like a duck is a duck.

A little white *canard* camouflages, shoots holes in truth.
Wendy, you tell lies like water takes to a duck.

SPACE TO FILL

"Your tooth's ready to fall out and I'll give you a nickel if you let me pull it."
My grandfather pinched the queen's face between thumb and index finger
while my baby tooth hung by a hinge
latched to gum and tasting of metal.

"Close the door real quick and you won't even feel it."
But I wouldn't let that little noose near my tooth.
"Don't be so damn childish," my mother said.
"You need to make some space in that mouth of yours."

He pulled his own teeth with pliers. "Dentists. Quacks. Shysters. Sonsofbitches."
He used an old sharpening stone to file down his dentures.
"See?" He held them like a crown. "The bastards finally fit properly."
But his mouth looked a little crooked now.

"The tooth fairy'll leave you a dime."
Even double-or-nothing didn't work.
My grandfather left with the nickel in his wallet
his distrust of dentists, and my tooth still intact.

I twisted out my own tooth watching Bugs Bunny bite a carrot
and ask me "What's up, doc?"
Now I had a hole in my mouth. Space to fill with hollow words pulled
from grown-up mouths.

THE HANGED MAN

my future foretold by a nuthatch
divining upside-down from its branch
that small bird haloed with yellow-green
was the hanged man in a T

this arrow-shaped nuthatch overturned
the trajectory of that afternoon
suspended between blue and crimson
sensing sky or blood on winter snow

I surrendered to a small bird
to the witching of the nuthatch
toward some ominous purgatory
reading its claws and feathers like tarot

COYOTE

Two of us balanced on that hard-worn path
dividing Ada Boulevard's four-squares
from trees and scrub bush that slope toward the river
and you surprised me by looking so scrawny, so wanting.
I had expected you to be more the wolf,
instead you wore a dry scruff of hot afternoon.

Hesitating, you looked at me with cynical pity
then turned from the path, shaking off the city.

ECHOES

A FAUN IN THE AFTERNOON

Nijinsky's ghost appeared in a green wood
against Bakst's set with its dancing gold
in the afternoon when the leaves shivered like a scarf
and the drummer heard Debussy's haunted tone

when the leaves danced like a scarf
the drummer haunted Debussy
whose ghost was gold against Bakst's set
Nijinsky appeared in a green wood in the afternoon

as the drummer shivered in a green wood
Nijinsky's ghost danced with a scarf
and Bakst's set haunted the leaves in the afternoon
and the drummer heard Debussy's gold tone

Debussy haunted the drummer
Nijinsky danced with Bakst's ghost
in the afternoon shivering and set with gold
the faun appeared in a green wood

ROTHKO CAME BACK IN FEBRUARY

when red blue yellow lights were still
on a string wound round a bleached lichen-covered rail
and a band of snow was a layer of resignation

Rothko came back as Junko and considered
his untitled paintings looking as if he was
his later works or triptychs in his chapel

black and gradually grey subtracting colour
his feathers melted into shadow or white snow
becoming all things and mixture of things

February is the heart's most brutal month
every four years it adds a day to itself
prolonging its feathered dark days

Rothko Junko told me:
from three colours you can make any colour
and everything can be replaced with nothing

EDITH SCHIELE: A CARDINAL REDRESSED

Egon's *Kneeling Female in Orange-Red Dress* was me.
Heavy or light as the substance of feathers and linen skies.
With dead leaves in my mouth and my weight chalked and painted
foregrounded face and seed-eye trapped in pose and repose.

I have met my *doppelgänger*: this northern cardinal redressed
crested wing-wrapped and wearing my seed-eye.
She is a claw on that tree's fingerbone
the flume of my respectable cunt.

Once the sick moon was eclipsed
by cadmium trailing a black thread.
A cardinal-inked sky sang quick come quick.
Egon drawing on my death bed.

It is October 28th. Look at me, don't look at me, you knotted painted bird.
I will keep this warm red turning in my mouth until you go.

VERMEER'S WOMAN IN BLUE READING A LETTER (A SHORT PLAY)

A Great Blue Heron is perched on one leg on a branch in an unidentified forest location. The green leaves around the Heron fade in and out of focus, from foreground to background. The Heron's expression is intense. But there is anticipation in its sharp yellow eyes, as if it is about to share a secret…

Heron:

Light rained on my head and on my beak and turned to ink
and on my wings the ink became the message that I sent
to you on a wing of waterfall sealed with a waxing blue moon
and a veined leaf. There is something I must tell you.

Woman in blue:

Is this for me or yourself? If you were only an object I could display you on a plinth for me to decipher. But you are a heron painted with an undercoat of water, blue that is uncontainable and unattainable. I am the woman swathed in muslin and reading the letter on fine vellum. This letter you sent only for me. A message coded in blue feathers and white light of water.

Heron:

When you get my letter don't tell Vermeer.
He will want to paint me, to capture me as
he has you. Capture my likeness, but it will be
a death mask. I am already here overpainted
and cloaked in my own light.
This letter is only for you, not for his
camera obscura. I must warn you…

AT THE BATHOUSE: NOVEMBER 18, 2018

The drummer set down his sticks and walked toward that silence.
Outside the studio, near the highway, he saw the gold-eyed owl and named it.
A downy hi-hat note resting on a worn wood-clef above an X of barbed wire.
Both emerged from somewhere pure, between music and indestructible matter.

Outside the studio, near the highway, he saw the gold-eyed owl and named it.
To see an owl in the daylight is a good omen, the drummer had been told.
Both emerged from somewhere pure, between music and indestructible matter.
Truth be told, it had been foretold in the beat of a drum and the words in a song.

To see an owl in the daylight is a good omen, the drummer had been told.
The owl and drummer were old and newborn at the same moment.
Truth be told, it had been foretold in the beat of a drum and the words in a song.
There are places I've never been and always wanted to go.

The owl and drummer were old and newborn at the same moment
A downy hi-hat note resting on a worn wood-clef above an X of barbed wire.
*There are places I've never been and always wanted to go.**
The drummer set down his sticks and walked toward that silence.

* "Fly" (Baker, Rob/Downie, Gord/Fay, Johnny/Langlois, Paul/Sinclair, Gord)

INFINITY AND A GUITAR

infinity terrified you when you were small
you needed certainty: beginning and end
years later we talk about the infinite
a guitar can make a sound that never dies

you needed certainty: beginning and end
with the break of a smooth wishbone
a guitar can make a sound that never dies
past pages and the inking of illuminated manuscripts

with the break of a smooth wishbone
an imaginary tuning fork tests a limit's limitations
past pages and the inking of illuminated manuscripts
that keeps the sound going beyond

an imaginary tuning fork tests a limit's limitations
the infinite guitar is not a theory: I accept its truth
that keeps the sound going beyond
street buskers playing endless electric and weary

the infinite guitar is not a theory: I accept its truth
in summer bees swarm the shrub by the front porch
street buskers playing endless electric and weary
like metal filings to a magnet circling the body and the neck

in summer bees swarm the shrub by the front porch
we call it by its nickname old man's walking stick
like metal filings to a magnet circling the body and the neck
the tree's Latin name is *Corylus avellana*

we call it by its nickname old man's walking stick
that *Sigma* guitar I bought you for Christmas
the tree's Latin name is *Corylus avellana*
you said you'd wanted a guitar like this forever

that *Sigma* guitar I bought you for Christmas
years later we talk about the infinite
you said you'd wanted a guitar like this forever
infinity terrified you when you were small

SWAN UPPING

A fat swan loved he best of any roost said Geoffrey of his monk amok with taboo taste for swan flesh. One-upping royalty. Swan upping. Count: one swan in Tommy Thompson Park. One nick or two. Knick-knack-nick-nought. This swan belongs to no one. Who's in charge of counting. Leslie Spit. Seven swans a-swimming given to someone somewhere someday somechristmas. Six swans were the silent woman's brothers. Knit six years six shirts the only way to turn them back. Count stitches. Risking a fire-tongued pyre she turns them all except one. Left with one wing and dreams of flying.

SING IN MANY POSITIONS

Some people are born with tissues muscles orifices superior to others. The voice of the ordinary can be improved. Imagine the voice is a little musical instrument, boxed up in Adam's apple.

Voice is the individual. The entire human being. Acquire an ideal carriage of the body. Become idealized. The singer must be fit. Better than the prizefighter. Call upon physical forces and vital powers.

Try to sing. Develop your body. Study singing to make a beautiful body. Sing in many positions – sitting, leaning, sometimes groveling.

Lean slightly forward upon one leg. Relax shoulders.
Chest high never rigid. Draw lower abdomen in without tension.

Assume a buoyancy, lightness, as though you were about to fly.

Found/redacted/manipulated from: "The Marvel of the Human Voice," page 723, by Oscar Saenger from *The Etude Music Magazine*, vol. XLIV, no. 10, October 1926. Theodore Presser Co., Philadelphia, Pa.

AUGURIES

That old scar beams its skeleton smile above my knee
parting skin like that broken toy box hinge did back then.
It took a while to bleed, the sharp corner made such a clean laceration.
This was before my fall from the high wooden steps to the clothesline.
Sometimes sparrows perched on it like little clothespins. I saw two
and fell to the concrete. Hard. It took a while to start crying.

These were auguries.
Now I don't count sparrows in our front yard hedge.
They are just the multitudinous shadows of the pair I saw when I was a child.
On winter mornings those shadows are singing their hurly-burly song.
When white light accedes, I know it comes down to this:
a struggle of stabbing beaks and flustering wings.

A CHICKADEE

breathes an epistle to the sapless winter branch
and with cursive claws inscribes a prayer
onto every dead flower
stamping each one with a red seal
signing and singing its name
haunting the bitter tasting air.

I WAS ALMOST ROBIN

With my bow and arrow,
I killed Cock Robin.

FROM THE TRADITIONAL ENGLISH NURSERY RHYME,
"WHO KILLED COCK ROBIN?"

Who killed cock robin? My mother broke it to me
with the first line of a nursery rhyme murder mystery.

What is it about that name: Robin? Your sacrament so well
sung with a book and blood-bowl. This rite a writer's dying to tell.

When winter's fading who do I wait for? You and your red breast.
Your defrosted chirpy riff. I still love to hate an optimist.

Where, then, did you go after leaving that nest of scraps
in our failing apple tree? I guess a home has its own kind of traps.

Why, your name could have been mine, but my father said no.
Wendy, I'll teach you to whistle. Here, purse your lips and blow.

THE BEAUTY OF VULTURES

If you cannot be seduced by beauty,
you cannot learn the wisdom of ugliness.
FROM *NOTES ON THOUGHT AND VISION*, H.D.

vultures can't sing but when they strike a triad
on this grey tin roof the middle vulture spreads its wings
across an octave of gizzard-ground-gruntings

I am pulled toward the ugly – my first imaginings
were faces of monsters and trolls and crones
in fairy tales my mother fed me from the one book we owned

like a vulture's featherless head – this book had no cover
but my mother and I scavenged from its insides
the beautiful and doomed the ugly and snide

vultures vomit-feed their chicks
what's digested gritty and made useful – it sticks
so memories of decay wisely used carry on

RAVEN

> *Shadow-maker create me everywhere*
> *Dark spaces (your face is my chosen abyss),*
> *For I said I have come to possess your darkness,*
> *Only this.*
>
> "THE SHADOW MAKER," GWENDOLYN MACEWEN

make me your perched shadow in daylight or night
make me the absence of all colour
make me the intaglio image behind your eye
make me that space where what you think you see is not
make me a nest of broken sticks and intellect
make me the simple universe inside an egg
Shadow-maker create me everywhere

A black rotary telephone dialing over and over.
An empty box.
A top hat.
A closet with a closed door.
Nowhere and everywhere.
Under the bed. Hide.
Dark spaces (your face is my chosen abyss)

Stop. Watch. Now you watch me.
Your raven-eye charts the path of nebulae
and I want to fall to follow the secrets of dead stars
their supple afterlife shining into my dreams again.
It's you, raven, after all. It's always you
calling and clicking and cawing WHAT WHAT WHAT
For I said I have come to possess your darkness

I consider the needle, ink my skin with your face
your beak feathers claws across my shoulders
so when I stretch out my arms I will feel your wings
spread in flight your head edging toward the wind
the stuff of teeth and nails have some chance to change me
into your darkness a sleek amalgam of cheek and genius.
I want only this my raven shadow-maker, to be you, shadow-maker
Only this.

acknowledgements

WENDY McGRATH:

This project has been a long time in the making — thank you Danny Miles for inspiring me with your haunting and beautiful photographs and for your continued enthusiasm for *The Beauty of Vultures.*

I'd also like to thank my editors, Thea Bowering and Jumoke Verissimo, for their sensitivity toward this book and their enthusiasm for this collaborative project.

Thank you to the staff at NeWest Press: Matt Bowes, Meredith Thompson, Carolina Ortiz, and Christine Hassay Kohler.

To my sons, Eamon and Brendan, thank you for your inspiration and for the joy your music has brought into my life.

Thank you to the anonymous donor who made it possible for me to receive the inaugural Prairie Grindstone Prize.

Finally, thanks to my husband, John, for his unwavering support of everything and anything I do.

Several poems in the manuscript have already been published (or exhibited) and include:

"A Barn Swallow Relative to Objects and Places." In *You Look Good for Your Age: an Anthology*, University of Alberta Press, 2021.

"Rothko Came Back in February." Blindman Brewing Beer Can stories, 2019.

"At the Bathouse: November 18, 2018." Displayed with Danny Miles' photograph of a snowy owl. Museum London exhibition of JUNO winners' photography from the past 40 years, presented in conjunction with the 2019 JUNO Awards.

"The Crooked Bush" and "Infinity and a Guitar." *Grain Magazine* 45, no. 2 (Winter 2018).

"A Faun in the Afternoon." In *Heartwood: Poems for the Love of Trees*, League of Canadian Poets, 2018.

DANNY MILES:

I would like to thank nature for being pure in an otherwise plastic world.

WENDY McGRATH is a Métis poet, writer, and visual artist living in amiskwacîwâskahikan (Edmonton) on Treaty 6 Territory and Métis Nation of Alberta Region 4. Winner of the inaugural Prairie Grindstone Prize 2023-2024, McGrath's writing practice embraces multiple genres – fiction, poetry, spoken word, and creative non-fiction. Her most recent hybrid publication, *The Orange Scribbler* (JackPine Press 2023) is a chapbook/artist's book inspired by heirloom recipes. McGrath describes her writing as "Prairie Gothic," and strives to give voice to working-class stories.

McGrath has published six books – four novels and two books of poetry. *Broke City* (NeWest Press), the final book in her Santa Rosa Trilogy (which includes *North East* and *Santa Rosa*), is a prairie gothic novel. Her two books of poetry, *A Revision of Forward* (NeWest Press) and *common place ecstasies* (Beach Holme Publishing) explore a range of poetic forms and approaches. Her work has been widely published in literary magazines such as *Grain*, and *Prairie Fire*, and anthologies such as *Beyond the Food Court* (Laberinto Press), *You Look Good for Your Age*, (University of Alberta Press), *Waiting* (University of Alberta Press), *Sweet Water: Poems for the Watershed* (Caitlin Press), and *Heartwood: Poems for the Love of Trees* (League of Canadian Poets).

McGrath's most recent spoken word project, "Before We Knew" (Entity Records), is her second collaboration with musician and producer, Sascha Liebrand. Her first spoken word project, "BOX," is an adaptation of McGrath's eponymous long poem with the group Quarto & Sound. "Movement 1" was nominated for a 2018 City of Edmonton Music Award in the Jazz Recording of the Year category.

Her work in the visual arts includes print making and artists books. In addition to *The Beauty of Vultures*, her collaborations with other visual artists, include "Avebury," an artist's book produced by Penrose Press, and inspired by McGrath's poems, and *A Revision of Forward* (NeWest Press) which was a print and poetry collaboration with renowned Edmonton-based print maker Walter Jule exhibited in Houston, Texas and Edmonton.

Wendy's contributions to the Canadian writing community are significant. Through mentoring, teaching, and active participation in literary events, she continues to foster the growth of countless writers and enrich the literary landscape. She has a Master of Arts, English, from York University. Her scholarly work has explored the Prairie Gothic genre.

Currently, McGrath is working on a new novel, poetry manuscript, and other projects.

DANNY MILES is a photographer, hip hop producer, and drummer for alt rock band July Talk. He is based in Toronto, Ontario. Instagram: @dannyptmiles

In 2017, to honour NeWest Press' 40th anniversary, we inaugurated a new poetry series to go alongside our Nunatak First Fiction, Prairie Play, and Writer as Critic series: Crow Said Poetry. Crow Said is named in honour of Robert Kroetsch's foundational 1977 novel *What The Crow Said*. The series aims to shed light on places and people outside of the literary mainstream. It is our intention that the poets featured in this series will continue Robert Kroetsch's literary tradition of innovation, interrogation, and generosity of spirit.

CROW SAID POETRY TITLES AVAILABLE FROM NEWEST

Tar Swan — David Martin

That Light Feeling Under Your Feet — Kayla Geitzler

Paper Caskets — Emilia Danielewska

let us not think of them as barbarians — Peter Midgley

Lullabies in the Real World — Meredith Quartermain

The Response of Weeds: A Misplacement of Black Poetry on the Prairies — Bertrand Bickersteth

Coconut — Nisha Patel

rump + flank — Carol Harvey Steski

How to Hold a Pebble — Jaspreet Singh

Kink Bands — David Martin

Attic Rain — Samantha Jones

Dreams of the Epoch & the Rock — Jaspreet Singh

The Beauty of Vultures — Wendy McGrath & Danny Miles